The Printer in Eighteenth-Century Williamsburg

An Account of His Life & Times, & of His Craft

Parke Rouse, (Editor: Thomas K. Ford)

Alpha Editions

This edition published in 2024

ISBN 9789362516640

Design and Setting By
Alpha Editions
www.alphaedis.com
Email - info@alphaedis.com

Contents

The Printer in Eighteenth-Century Williamsburg

The paragraphs on this Page and the next have been ſet in an eighteenth-century Manner. The Type uſed is *Caſlon*, developed in the early Part of the eighteenth Century by *William Caſlon*, the greateſt of the Engliſh Letter Founders. *Caſlon* in 1734 iſſued his firſt Broadſide Specimen Sheet of Type Faces cut at his Foundry during the preceding Decade and a Half.

Although *Caſlon* is famous for the beautiful Type that bears his Name, he deſerves equal Credit for deſigning ſome of the moſt handſome Type Ornaments or "Flowers" ever developed, before or after his Time. Such Type Flowers had many Uſes—to embelliſh Initial Letters at the Beginning of a Chapter in a Book; as decorative Devices in a ſingle Row over a Type Heading ſtarting a new Page in a Book; or over Headings each Time a new Subject was introduced in a Text. Flowers were caſt to all the regular Bodies of the Letter from the ſmall (*Nonpareil*) to the large (*Great Primer*) Size. The Type Flowers uſed at the Head of this Page, in the built-up Initial opening the firſt Paragraph, and elſewhere in this Publication are reproduced from original eighteenth-century Flowers excavated at the Site of the Printing Office on *Duke of Glouceſter* Street in *Williamſburg*.

The longs "s" ſo evident in theſe Paragraphs originated in the *German* Hand Script. Early *German* Type Founders attempted to reproduce Handwriting as cloſely as poſſible. In the Attempt the long "s" was evolved and was adopted by the firſt *Engliſh* Printers who learned their Trade from the *Germans*. The long "s" remained in general Uſe until about the Year 1800. It was always uſed at the Beginning and in the Middle of a Word, but never to terminate a Word. It can eaſily be recognized by the Fact of having only half a Croſſbar or none at all, whereas the Letter "f" has a full Croſſbar.

Ligatures, ſuch as ct, ſb, ſſ, ſi, ſſi, ſk, ſl, ſſl, ſt, fi, ffi, ff, fl, ffl, were developed where a long "s" or an "f" overlapped the following Letter. Caſting the two Characters together avoided Damage to the overlapping Letter. Although ſome Ligatures have fallen into Diſuſe, the fi, ffi, ff, fl, and ffl are ſtill common today.

Printers alſo applied, through much of the Century, ſome Rules of Style which the modern Reader may find odd if not awkward. For Example, they began all Nouns with a capital Letter, thus diſtinguiſhing them from other Parts of Speech ſuch as Adjectives, Verbs, &c. In the ſame Faſhion, they capitalized Expreſſions of particular Emphaſis, and Titles of Honor and Eminence. The Names of Perſons and Places they not only began with capital Letters but usually ſet in *Italic* Type as well.

With the exception of certain *Scottiſh* faces, small Capitals were found in *Roman* Fonts of Type only. They were employed to denote Emphaſis and Streſs, and were uſed where the large Capitals would not fit, i.e., were too long. Small Capitals were alſo found in the firſt Word of the firſt Paragraph after every Break in Context of a Chapter or Section of Text.

Strange though ſome eighteenth-century Printing may appear to today's Reader, there is one Point that ſhould be ſtreſſed. The Idioſyncracies of a Type Page of the Period were not merely Whims of individual Printers. They were the Faſhion of the Time. When a Printer uſed ſeveral Sizes and Styles of Type on a Page, he was practicing what he and his Contemporaries conſidered to be good Typography.

If you had visited Williamsburg in the year 1743, say, and wanted to post a letter, buy a book, a newspaper, or some writing paper, or talk with an influential townsman, you would have sought out the shop of William Parks on Duke of Gloucester Street. Parks published the *Virginia Gazette*, the first newspaper in the Virginia colony, and his printing office served also as post office, bookshop, stationery store, and general information center.

It was a place of many sounds and smells, and of much activity. There you would find ink-smudged printer's devils carefully sorting type under the watchful eye of the journeyman printer, an accomplished craftsman and exacting instructor. There you would also find the bookbinder among his calfskins, marbled papers, glues, and presses. And on the shelves, waiting for buyers, were pamphlets and leatherbound volumes produced in the shop or imported from England.

Perhaps, if you were lucky, you might see a postrider burst in with London papers, rushed from a ship just arrived from England. Then the printing shop was never livelier, for the coming of news from abroad was an exciting event. At such times, Printer Parks probably stopped what he was doing, culled the choicest items from the London journals, and made space for them on the front page of the next issue of the *Gazette*. In a day or so, "the freshest Advices, Foreign and Domestick," would be on their way to Parks's subscribers.

In the small (1,500 people) capital of Williamsburg, this printing office was a nerve center through which news of the vast outer world reached Virginians and, in turn, news of His Majesty's largest American colony was conveyed to other colonists and their homeland. By modern standards it was a small printing shop. But in its effect on the people of the Virginia colony, it was a powerful civilizing force. As one of eight or nine printers of colonial newspapers, moreover, William Parks, through his paper, kept the people of the other colonies informed of the major events that were taking place in the oldest and largest outpost of Britain in America.

THE PRINTING OFFICE TODAY

For these reasons, Colonial Williamsburg has re-created an eighteenth-century printing office as one of its series of craft shops. Here the twentieth-century visitor will find equipment such as was used two hundred years ago in similar printing establishments on Duke of Gloucester Street operated by Parks and later by William Hunter, Joseph Royle, Alexander Purdie, John Dixon, William Hunter, Jr., William Rind, and their successors. Here a master printer and his apprentice, in the leather aprons and full-cut breeches of the period, set by hand type closely resembling that which Parks used.

To print its pages of hand-set type, the present Printing Office has in operation three so-called "English Common Presses" such as were built in the eighteenth century. One, believed to have been made about 1750, was given to Colonial Williamsburg by American Type Founders, Incorporated, and the Rochester Institute of Technology. Of the other two, one was designed by Ralph Green of Chicago after a careful study of the handful of known eighteenth-century presses in the United States, and both were built by Colonial Williamsburg craftsmen.

In addition to the *Gazette*, tracts, pamphlets, and books poured from Parks's press from the time he came to Williamsburg about 1730 until he died on a voyage to England in 1750. Surviving examples of his work reveal that he first used Dutch type, which was followed by the more pleasing face so "friendly to the eye" developed by William Caslon in England. From matrices similar to Caslon's originals, his successors in the type-founding business have cast the letters used on the restored Williamsburg press. Parks's neat printing and binding ornaments, so characteristic of the classical-minded eighteenth century, have been similarly reproduced. Eighteenth-century printers' tools were made from the careful drawings in Diderot's Encyclopedia and from other sources.

To provide the kind of paper used by eighteenth-century printers, Colonial Williamsburg began research in the 1930s into the history of the town's only paper mill. Started by Parks about 1743 with the help of his friend Benjamin Franklin, the mill is believed to have outlived him. Examples of its product were identified in 1936 in a German Bible and a song book printed in Pennsylvania in 1763. Paper that simulated the Parks paper was thereupon reproduced, and was used in some of the work of the Printing Office and in some Colonial Williamsburg books designed after examples of Parks's work. Even the specks and spots of the original Parks paper were imitated by a mixture of ground flaxseed incorporated into the paper to insure the appearance of authenticity.

Visitors to the Printing Office today may not see counterparts of the postriders who brought mail to Parks's printing shop and post office, but nearly everything else is there. As in colonial days, the central figure is still the printer, bending over his press and producing in a day's work what one modern, mechanized press can turn out in a few minutes.

WILLIAMSBURG'S FIRST PRINTER

Although the colony of Virginia was founded in 1607, it was not until the eighteenth century that printing was established there. This delay was largely due to governmental policy. In seventeenth-century England and her colonies, freedom of the press was yet to be established. Even laws passed by governing bodies could not without official permission be printed and circulated for the benefit of citizens. Until the Licensing Act of 1662 expired in 1695, the printing trade in England was confined to London, the universities of Oxford and Cambridge, and to the English city of York. The governors of the royal colony of Virginia felt empowered to refuse permission for the establishment of printing until the year 1690, after which printers were governed by royal instructions which required a license and permission from the governor as a prerequisite to setting up shop.

Sir William Berkeley, who was governor of Virginia from 1642 to 1652 and again from 1660 to 1677, summarized the attitude of most officials of his day in his famous statement, "But, I thank God, there are no free schools nor printing, and I hope we shall not have these hundred years; for learning has brought disobedience, and heresy, and sects into the world, and printing has divulged them, and libels against the best government. God keep us from both." (Berkeley was in error: free schools *had* existed in Virginia, though printing had not.)

In 1682, a few years after Berkeley wrote, a printer named William Nuthead came to Jamestown, then the capital of Virginia, proposing to serve the government by printing the acts of the Assembly. He was ordered by the Governor's Council to await royal approval. Several months later a new governor arrived with an order from the king that "no person be permitted to use any press for printing upon any occasion whatsoever." Nuthead moved to Maryland, and printing in Virginia was delayed fifty years.

Before 1730, however, a more tolerant attitude had developed. With the permission of Governor William Gooch, the English-born William Parks moved that year from Annapolis to Williamsburg, which had succeeded Jamestown as the capital of Virginia in 1699. He was designated public printer of Virginia, at an annual salary of £120 a year, eventually increased to £280. Parks continued to print the acts of the Virginia Assembly, which he had begun several years before in Maryland, and soon advertised for subscriptions for a proposed *Virginia Miscellany* "at his House, near the Capitol, in Williamsburg." Before the year was out he had printed several works, at least five of which are known by title. One of these is an ode to printing, *Typographia*, by one "J. Markland," which salutes Gooch for his encouragement of printing. In the high-flown style of its day, the ode concludes:

"A Ruler's gentle Influence

Shall o'er his Land be shewn;

Saturnian Reigns shall be renew'd

Truth, Justice, Vertue, be pursu'd

Arts flourish, Peace shall crown the Plains,

Where GOOCH administers, AUGUSTUS reigns."

Parks was Williamsburg's most distinguished eighteenth-century printer and probably its most successful. In the annals of his craft in America he is ranked with Benjamin Franklin and William Bradford, the foremost printers in Pennsylvania and New York. Parks, like all of his brethren, depended for his bread and butter on printing blank forms (deeds, mortgages, bills, and the like), government work (such as proclamations, forms, and laws), almanacs, and other job work, but he helped establish in the American colonies that dependence upon free and fair discussion of issues in the newspapers which strengthened the concept of a free press. He gave impetus to literature in a colony that had lacked the local means for its encouragement. By his example, he was partly responsible for the rash of journalistic enterprise in pre-Revolutionary Williamsburg.

Parks's most influential act was his founding of the *Virginia Gazette*, the first newspaper to be published in Virginia and the second south of Maryland. Begun in 1736, this weekly was the leader of a colorful succession of similarly named sheets in Williamsburg and later in Richmond, to which the Virginia government removed in 1780. And in these *Gazettes*—in the 1770s published by as many as three competing printers at a time—can be found a rich chronicle of the events in the colonies leading to the American Revolution. Important foreign and domestic occurrences were described in dispatches— perhaps taken in some cases from private correspondence—and in excerpts from other newspapers. The editor rarely reported local happenings beyond a brief mention of ship arrivals, marriages, deaths, fires, and the like. He often printed legal notices and entire acts of the Virginia Assembly, without comment. Fulsomely phrased letters to the editor posed weighty questions of government, science, or theology.

The modern reader will find the *Virginia Gazette* of 1736 to 1750 undramatic in its lack of headlines, pictures, and display type.

But the ingredients of human interest are there, subtly in the note of controversy which gradually built up to the Revolution, and emphatically in the advertisements, which largely financed the *Gazette*. Many are the notices of runaway slaves, strayed farm animals, husbands deserted by wives, or blooded horses available for racing or breeding. From the advertisements, also, the contemporary Virginia reader could learn of the arrival of goods from London—articles of fashion that were highly prized by Virginians as evidence of their Englishness. In an early issue of the *Gazette*, Parks states:

"ADVERTISEMENT, concerning ADVERTISEMENTS

"ALL Persons who have Occasion to buy or sell Houses, Lands, Goods, or Cattle; or have Servants or Slaves Runaway; or have lost Horses, Cattle, &c. or want to give any Publick Notice; may have it advertis'd in all these *Gazettes* printed in one Week, for Three Shillings, and for Two Shillings *per* Week for as many Weeks afterwards as they shall order, by giving or sending their Directions to the *Printer* hereof.

"And, as these Papers will circulate (as speedily as possible) not only all over This, but also the Neighbouring Colonies, and will probably be read by some Thousands of People, it is very likely they may have the desir'd Effect; and it is certainly the cheapest and most effectual Method that can be taken, for Publishing any Thing of this Nature."

PRINTING IN AN AGRICULTURAL ECONOMY

William Parks's significant achievements seem even greater if one understands the difficulties of operating a business in the Williamsburg of 1730-1750. Because Virginia's colonial prosperity was based on a one-crop economy—tobacco—little "ready money" was in circulation within the colony. The weed itself became a sort of currency. The usual practice was for the plantation owner or the small farmer to subsist on his produce and his credit until the crop was harvested and shipped to English merchants, who from the proceeds of its sale bought for the planter such articles as he had directed. Because all American tobacco was transported to Britain in British vessels, shipping space was plentiful on the westward passage, and shipowners and British merchants offered Virginia buyers cheap freight rates on finished goods. Thus such English manufactures as cloth, furniture, pewter, silver, and ceramics were sold to Virginia planters and merchants.

The two-way trade between Virginia planters and British merchants slowed down the development of a large Virginia artisan group. Accordingly, local industry was limited in eighteenth-century Virginia, even in an urban center such as Williamsburg. Virginia craftsmen complained bitterly of unpaid accounts, the necessity of accepting such "country pay" as tobacco, corn, and beef, and the paucity of buyers who offered ready money.

It is easy to understand why William Parks found relatively few craftsmen in the Williamsburg of his day. Except for a few trades such as cabinetmaking, blacksmithing, coopering, wigmaking, tailoring, and shoemaking, the Virginia capital was largely a community of taverns, townhouses, and governmental institutions, and the colony itself was overwhelmingly rural. There is no doubt that Virginia's reliance on agriculture, a reliance approved by British mercantile theory, resulted in an overdependence on the industry of the mother country. We can thank the peculiarities of Parks's situation—the inability of English printers to satisfy Virginians' desire for regional news, and the subsidy Parks received as public printer—that his craft became firmly established in the 1730s in Virginia. Indeed, it seems clear that the prospect of becoming Virginia's public printer was what lured Parks from Annapolis to Williamsburg in the first place.

PARKS'S SUCCESSORS IN WILLIAMSBURG

Altogether, Williamsburg had at least twelve master printers and three separate printing locations or offices during the colonial period. After Parks died on a voyage to England, William Hunter, the man whom he had left in charge, bought the business. Publication of the *Virginia Gazette* continued, and Hunter became public printer and postmaster. In the latter capacity he worked in close association with an astute Philadelphia printer, Benjamin Franklin, with whom he served jointly as deputy postmaster-general for all the colonies. Hunter printed in 1754 the first published writing of George Washington, entitled *The Journal of Major George Washington, sent by the Hon. Robert Dinwiddie, Esq; His Majesty's Lieutenant-Governor, and Commander in Chief of Virginia, to the Commandant of the French Forces on Ohio....*

After Hunter's death in 1761, the printing office had a succession of owners and operators. As tension increased between Great Britain and her American colonies, especially after the adoption of the Stamp Act in 1765, the relation of public printer to government became more difficult. The printer faced the necessity of maintaining good relations with both loyalist and patriot elements in the House of Burgesses. One loyalist reader of the *Gazette*, the Reverend John Camm, complained in the early 1760s that Hunter's successor, Joseph Royle, refused to publish Camm's pamphlet arguing the cause of Church of England clergymen because of its "Satyrical Touches upon the Late Assembly." On the other hand, certain patriot members criticized Royle in the columns of the *Maryland Gazette* for allegedly refusing to print their criticisms of local government. The printer was caught between fires.

Criticism of the *Gazette* continued after Royle died in January 1766, and Alexander Purdie, a Scotsman, took over the business. In what is thought to have been his first issue, Purdie announced that "the press shall likewise be as free as any Gentleman can wish, or desire; and I crave the countenance and favour of the publick no longer than my conduct may appear to merit their approbation." Later the same month, Purdie wrote, "As I understand it is thought by some that I have neglected, or refused, to publish the account of a late transaction at Hobb's Hole [Tappahannock], this is to assure the publick ... that I never saw the same, nor was it ever offered to me to publish, otherwise it would have seen the light before this time: For I do now, as I have heretofore declared, that my press shall be as free as any Gentleman can wish or desire; that is, as free as any publick press upon the continent." In 1775, after Purdie established another *Virginia Gazette*, his paper bore the appealing motto "Always for Liberty, and the Publick Good."

TOWARD A FREE PRESS

In spite of Purdie's efforts, the trend was toward a competitive press. A rival *Virginia Gazette* was set up in Williamsburg in 1766 by William Rind, a Maryland printer who was more sympathetic to the protesting colonists than Royle and Purdie were thought to be. The motto of his paper cannily proclaimed "Open to all Parties but influenced by None." Governor Francis Fauquier at this time reported to the British Board of Trade: "The late printer to the Colony [Royle] is dead, and as the press was then thought to be too complaisant to me, some of the hot Burgesses invited a printer [Rind] from Maryland. Upon which the foreman [Purdie] to the late printer, who is also a candidate for the place, has taken up the newspaper again in order to make interest with the Burgesses." Jefferson, who in 1766 was completing his study of law, and was a friend and admirer of Fauquier's, recalled later: "We had but one press, and that having the whole business of the government, and no competitor for public favor, nothing disagreeable to the governor could be got into it. We procured Rind to come from Maryland to publish a free paper."

The hot-spirited Rind was elected public printer by the House of Burgesses. However, the job being too much for one printer alone, the Assembly in 1769 authorized both *Gazette* publishers, Rind and Purdie, to print a large volume containing the Acts of Assembly then in force. Rind continued in office until his death in 1773 when his widow, Clementina Rind, took over the business as Virginia's first woman printer.

The number of weekly newspapers in Williamsburg increased again in 1775 when Purdie, who had taken John Dixon into his business nine years before, withdrew in favor of William Hunter, Jr., the son of William Parks's successor, and established his own *Virginia Gazette.* When the Revolution broke in 1776, Williamsburg thus had three newspapers, each called the *Virginia Gazette.* Rind's *Gazette* expired by 1777, after a succession of managers, and Purdie's (which was continued after his death in 1779 by Clarkson and Davis) ceased publication in 1780. Dixon formed a new partnership with Thomas Nicolson in 1779 after William Hunter, Jr., had joined the British forces. Their newspaper was called the *Phoenix Gazette and Williamsburg Intelligencer,* but it expired the following year when these printers followed the seat of government to establish Richmond's first press.

So pronounced was the decline in Williamsburg's fortunes that from the year of the government's removal until forty-four years later, in 1824, Williamsburg had no newspaper. Old copies of the three *Gazettes* were treasured reminders of the town's past glory. The name, *Virginia Gazette,* and some of the tradition of Parks's skill were remembered, but little was done to perpetuate them until the late Dr. W. A. R. Goodwin in 1926 invited Mr. John D. Rockefeller, Jr., to restore Williamsburg. As a by-product of that movement, the proud masthead of William Parks's original *Virginia Gazette* was revived in 1930 by the late Joseph A. Osborne and his family. Likewise, in the realm of paper manufacture, typography, book production, and bookbinding, Colonial Williamsburg has revived the workmanship of William Parks and his confreres. In such publications as *The Williamsburg Art of Cookery, or, Accomplish'd Gentlewoman's Companion,* published in 1938, and *A Brief & True Report concerning Williamsburg in Virginia,* first published in 1935, Colonial Williamsburg emulated type, paper, format, and binding of similar volumes from Parks's press. And at its Printing Office, it has sought to recapture the manner and mood of a colonial printing shop as a part of its program to teach twentieth-century Americans more about the lives and ideas of their pre-Revolutionary ancestors.

TECHNIQUES OF EIGHTEENTH-CENTURY PRINTING

In considering the craft of printing, it is important to remember that the western world has enjoyed the invention of movable type only since the middle of the fifteenth century. For several centuries thereafter, the new development was regarded with suspicion by church and state, which, as we have seen, feared the freedom of thought that would ensue if reading matter were readily available. Even in the eighteenth century, an era of enlightenment, printing was suspect.

An equally difficult obstacle facing the colonial printer was the cost of his press, his type, his paper, and his equipment. Eighteenth-century industry was largely home operated, based on the capital and ingenuity of one family. Yet the cost of equipping even the modest one- or two-press shops of eighteenth-century America was a burden for most people of the working class. In his famous *Autobiography,* Benjamin Franklin gives a vivid picture of the immense labor and thought that lay between a printer's apprenticeship and ownership. To reach the level of success that Franklin and Parks achieved required not only skill but unusual industry and shrewdness.

Eighteenth-century appraisals of several printing houses indicate an average value of £100 to £125 currency. We may suppose that William Parks set up shop in Williamsburg in 1730 on some such scale as this, adding type and other equipment to the value of £359 Virginia currency or £288 sterling at the time his equipment was sold to William Hunter in 1751. Undoubtedly Parks's three presses and his type constituted his chief equipment. The presses presumably were of the English common sort, which had then been in standard use in the

British Isles for nearly one hundred years. The type was an alloy of lead, tin, and antimony, the letters having been cast in Holland or England, and probably was valued at more than the rest of Parks's facilities together. For the rest, equipment consisted of such printers' staples as poles for drying paper, "shooting sticks," quoins, planes, type cases, type racks, composing sticks, lye troughs, wetting troughs, and other paraphernalia. For bookbinding the printer needed other instruments, some of which could be made in Williamsburg. The majority of the tools, however, were imported from Great Britain or Holland.

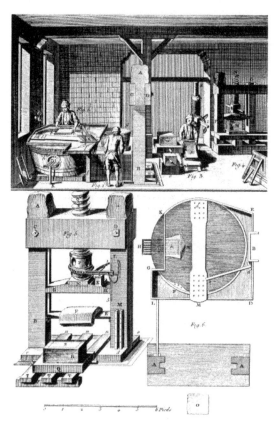

A paper mill. Here are shown the operations involved in making a sheet of paper in the eighteenth century. (1) The vatman dipping the deckle and screen into a vat of paper pulp. (2) The coucher removing the deckle and pressing the freshly formed sheet of paper on felt. (3) Preparing the new paper for pressing. (4) A rack for stacking wet

As he received each font or size of type, the colonial printer would distribute it in a set of four wooden trays, two for Roman type and two for italic. These contained partitions for each "character," or "sort," as the letters and numerals were called. Such partitions varied in size depending on the frequency of use of each letter or numeral, and they were so placed as to permit the printer to assemble type with a minimum of movement. (Because capital letters are usually arranged in the upper two cases and small letters in the lower two, printers traditionally refer to them as "upper case" or "lower case," respectively.)

In setting a page of printed matter the colonial printer rapidly plucked the necessary characters, one by one, from their compartments in the upper and lower cases. He placed them, with proper spacing, in a "composing stick" set to the proper length of line. When the stick was full he transferred the type to a shallow wooden tray called a "galley." Having assembled in the galley enough type to form a page, the printer "tied it off," i.e., bound a piece of string tightly around the whole mass. Then he could slide the assembled page off the galley onto the surface of the "imposing stone," a flat marble working surface. Such transfers of type—especially from composing stick to galley— were often attended with accidents. One of the printer's commoner frustrations was to have a stick, a galley, or even a whole page form of type dropped and "pied."

On the imposing stone a rectangular wrought-iron frame or "chase" was then placed around the type, and the finished page was locked into place with wooden blocks and wedges called "furniture" and "quoins." After being locked, it could be picked up and moved to the printing press without danger of the type falling out of place.

The eighteenth-century printer used paper made by hand from linen rags, importing it from Great Britain in the earlier years while domestic mills were gradually developing. Because such paper was uneven in texture and poorly sized, it was dampened before being put on the press to provide a more pliant working surface. For ink, Parks and his contemporaries used a combination of lampblack and varnish, which remain the chief constituents of printer's ink today. Lampblack was obtained by burning various materials and collecting the carbon in flues, while varnish was made of pine resin boiled in linseed oil until a clear liquid resulted. Most printers "rubbed" or mixed the lampblack and varnish thoroughly. If the mixture was too thick, it could be thinned with linseed oil or whale oil. If red ink was desired for two-color printing, vermilion could be substituted for lampblack.

A view of a typical eighteenth-century printer's composing room. Here type was set by hand to be printed on the press. (1) Setting type in a composing stick. (2) Transferring a stick of set type to a galley. (3) Planing a type form by beating lightly on the type surface with a block of wood and a mallet. DIDEROT.

A typical press room. The puller and beater are shown in two stages of the operations. On the left, a sheet of paper is placed on the tympan by the puller, and the type is inked by the beater. On the right, the puller is printing an impression on the paper, and the beater is distributing ink on his stocks while he inspects the previous pull. DIDEROT.

Once the printer or his apprentices had set the type, pulled a proof, "made up" the type into pages with the proper spacing and ornaments, and then locked it into forms by means of furniture and quoins, he placed his form on the press and adjusted it to get the most even impression. Then he was ready to begin the actual process of printing. Whereas printing is commonly done today by automatic presses, fed with paper either mechanically or by hand, it had to be done one sheet at a time in the eighteenth century. Two men usually worked the press, and the printing of a single impression required approximately a dozen different manual operations.

To ink his press, preparatory to printing, the "beater" spread the necessary amount of ink on his mixing block and rubbed it to an even consistency—that of stiff molasses—with a wooden brayer. With two leather-covered balls attached to wooden handles, he then collected ink from the stone, beat the "ink balls" together to distribute the sticky fluid over their surfaces, and then with a rapid rocking and rolling motion, transferred it onto the type. Then the "puller" placed his paper on a skin-covered wooden frame called a tympan and folded over it another light covered frame, called a frisket. These two frames in turn folded down onto the bed of the press, where the type was locked in its iron form or chase.

The actual impression was made by rolling the bed of the press, complete with folded tympan and frisket, beneath the platen, which was suspended from a large metal screw. By applying the force of the screw, the puller pressed the paper firmly against the inked type. The size of the printed matter might vary from a small bookplate or lottery ticket to a sheet twelve by eighteen inches, which was roughly the page size of Purdie and Dixon's *Virginia Gazette* of 1759. Whatever the dimension, the beater had to ink his form and the puller had to close and open his press again each time a surface was printed. Since the platen was so small, only one-half of a two-page wide newspaper could be printed at a time on the early press, and a repeat operation was required to complete one side of the sheet. Thus the press was sometimes called a "two-pull" press.

Two experienced pressmen, working at full speed, could turn out a "token" or 240 printed sheets (with two pulls and on one side only) per hour. Such a speed could not long be maintained; the practical output was closer to 200 sheets per hour. But wages were low, working hours were long, and the printer could keep his force on the job until the work was done.

THE PRINTER AND HIS MEN

Because of its close association with literature, the craft of printing has generally attracted a more intellectual type of craftsman and enjoyed a prestige greater than most others. Over the centuries, master printers have jealously enforced the standards of their predecessors, insisting today, as in the eighteenth century, on a long apprenticeship for learners. Upon completion of the stipulated learning period and achievement of the required proficiency, the apprentice then, as now, became a journeyman. A mature and experienced worker at this stage, he was qualified to take his leave of his master, if he desired, and to practice his craft where he wished. When such a printer engaged in work for himself and employed others, he became a master printer.

The apprentice system was in some respects a great boon to eighteenth-century craftsmen, for it provided cheap labor in return only for training and the necessities of life. Each master took into his establishment a number of youngsters, hoping that some might prove of "bright genius and good disposition." To these he obligated himself to provide food, shelter, and in most cases, clothing. The apprentice thereupon became a member of the printer's household, performing any chores assigned to him in the home, shop, or printing office. But although apprentice labor was cheap, it was unskilled and often inept. Apprenticeships were frequently broken off, and only the relatively few youths who were suited for the work and desirous of learning the "art and mystery" of the craft kept at it until accepted as journeymen at the age of twenty-one.

Many accounts have come down to us of the abuses as well as the uses of the apprentice system. Runaways were frequent, as attested by advertisements such as the one William Parks ran in the *Virginia Gazette* in 1745 for the return of a "smooth-tongued" apprentice "who makes Locks, and is dexterous at picking them." Sometimes mere children were apprenticed by poorer families who were unable to support them. Isaiah Thomas, a New England printer, was indentured at the age of six. In return for his training and keep, he bound himself to avoid drunkenness and carnal pursuits and to serve his master until he became twenty-one. However, the majority of apprentices were indentured at fourteen, to serve until they reached man's estate.

The apprentice system largely supplied the printer's need for unskilled labor, but he could supplement it with slaves or with indentured servants. The latter were usually young Englishmen of the lower classes who had emigrated to America and who had bound themselves to a term of labor in return for their voyage. Unlike apprentices, however, they were not required to be taught to print.

Trained, or journeymen, printers were scarce in colonial times, and they seem to have been often on the go. Even master printers moved about frequently. William Parks had engaged in printing in three English towns and in Annapolis before coming to Williamsburg in 1730. William Rind, who established his paper in Williamsburg in 1766, came there from Annapolis. Of Williamsburg's other master printers and journeymen, some were locally trained but others had been apprenticed in England.

A NOTE ON THE PRINTING OFFICE

Although the Printing Office of Colonial Williamsburg does not attempt precisely to re-create any particular colonial printing shop, it does represent the craft as it was practiced in the mid-1700s. Here the twentieth-century American is invited to pause and look about him. Perhaps, if he is in a receptive mood, he may sense the spirit of the talented William Parks, keeping a watchful eye over apprentices and journeymen while type is set, presses are inked, and impressions are pulled from the press. Perhaps he can discern some Virginia planter making his way to Parks's bookshelf, to buy Allestree's *The Whole Duty of Man* or Bayly's *The Practice of Piety* to take with him to his plantation and read during winter evenings.

Entering the Printing Office, the visitor finds himself in a typical Williamsburg structure of the eighteenth century. Fireplaces on each floor of the shop warm the workers in cold weather and dry the printed sheets of paper hung on overhead racks. Many-paned windows provide most of the shop's illumination during daylight hours, and also a place—in the bays on Duke of Gloucester Street—for the printer to post signs and samples of his work. At night and on dark days candelabra hanging from the ceiling and tin sconces against the walls hold candles whose smoky flames blacken the plaster as they help to light the working areas.

On the street floor are the post office, stationery, and bookselling counter—one of the important areas of the normal colonial printing office, since it combined three of the most important sidelines. Along with the shelves of books for sale, some bound in leather and some in temporary paper covers, there is a mail rack with slots for letters and newspapers.

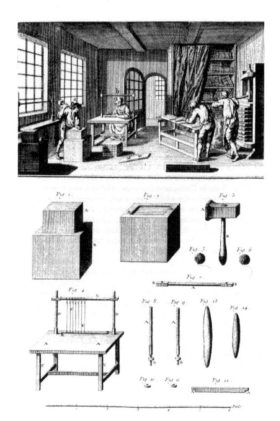

A bookbindery. In this view, several important binding operations can be seen. (a) Beating folded sections of a book so that they will lie flat. (b) Stitching folded sections to the heavy cords that hold the book together. (c) Trimming the edges of a freshly sewn book on a

ploughing press. (d) Pressing freshly bound books in a large standing press. BELOW. (1-3) The blocks and hammer used by the binder. (4) The sewing frame. (5-6) Twine. (7-12) Parts of the sewing frame. (13-14) Wood or bone folders. DIDEROT.

On the same floor is the printer's "counting room" or what would nowadays be called his "accounting department." Here he kept the numerous business records called for by the cumbersome bookkeeping systems of that day, penned business letters, and perhaps wrote out in longhand the material he intended for publication in the *Virginia Gazette*. Eighteenth-century printers often engaged in several other businesses at the same time—importing goods of almost any kind, selling farm products on commission, and trying anything that might turn a penny.

Excavation of the Printing Office site and careful study of the surviving eighteenth-century foundations and brick flooring gave evidence—in the form of reinforced footings—as to where at least one press may have stood. This was in the lower floor of the building, where again today the shop's printing operation is concentrated. There the three presses mentioned earlier occupy the center of the room, all of them in working order. Large racks for the storage of type line the wall, surmounted by open, slanting cases of type in current use. The cases contain a complete set of Caslon letters, from the diminutive Nonpareil (6-point) to Six Line Pica (72-point), which is one inch tall. Usually the printer employs the Pica (12-point) and English (14-point) sizes, which were customarily used in colonial times. He and his colleagues identified type sizes by name only; since the present point system was not in use then.

Printer's ink and its ingredients—varnish, lampblack or vermilion, and linseed oil—are kept in saltglaze jugs. Other vessels contain drinking water, and the wetting trough is filled, ready for dampening paper before printing. On the floor, weighted boards atop stacks of wetted paper keep the sheets from curling as the dampness permeates evenly throughout the pile.

Here the printer and his helpers set type, pull proofs and correct their galleys, make up pages on the marble imposing stone, prepare paper and ink, run off the job on one or more of the presses, and finally, redistribute the type to the cases. The printed sheets, in the meantime, may have to be hung on ceiling racks to allow both ink and paper to dry out.

In the small back shop, a separate building, the similarly cluttered bookbinding shop may be found. In it the bookbinder of today, working with the tools and methods of his eighteenth-century predecessors, sews together the printed and folded signatures that make a book, binds them in boards, and covers the boards—perhaps in elegantly decorated leather bindings. He may use marbled paper of his own making for end-papers or on the outer covers of smaller books. For tooling and lettering the cover he has a collection of brass dies, some of which are designed from lettering stamps excavated in the vicinity of his—and William Parks's workshop.

OUR PRINTING HERITAGE

From the crude presses of Williamsburg came an ingredient essential to the movement toward American self-government and independence—the political pamphlet. In the world of the eighteenth century, devoid of radio, television, or the bulky daily paper, the substance of political debate came from such pamphlets. It was also an era which took its political philosophy seriously, and the author of a pamphlet could count on wide readership among the planter-aristocrats who controlled the machinery of government. Williamsburg, as the colony's capital and its political and intellectual center, was the obvious city to lend its imprint to the speculations of Virginia's pamphleteers.

One of the most significant early tracts was Richard Bland's *An Inquiry into the Rights of the British Colonies*, printed by Alexander Purdie in March 1766. Writing in the aftermath of the previous year's fiery Stamp Tax debates, Bland vigorously proclaimed his belief in Locke's doctrines of natural rights and natural law. Reprinted in London, Bland's tract was evidence of the mounting sentiment for self-rule in the colonies. Bland's *Inquiry* was also a memorial to its author, a man who devoted much of his life to public service. An aged delegate to Virginia's first state legislature in October 1776, Bland collapsed in the Williamsburg streets on his way to a session, and died hours later in the home of his friend, John Tazewell.

The most important pamphlet printed in Williamsburg was *A Summary View of the Rights of British America*, from the pen of Thomas Jefferson. Lying ill up-country in August of 1774, when Virginia's legislators were convened in Williamsburg to send off delegates for the First Continental Congress, Jefferson wrote his tract to suggest instructions that might guide these delegates at Philadelphia.

The *Summary View* was read aloud by Peyton Randolph in his home on Market Square to a room filled with Virginia patriots. It was too radical for some, but moving to all. It was at once set in type by Clementina Rind, Williamsburg's only woman printer. Among the first to purchase a copy was George Washington, who noted in his diary that it cost him three shillings ninepence. The pamphlet was reprinted in Philadelphia and London and has been described as second only to the Declaration of Independence in charting the American course toward independence. John Adams of Massachusetts testified that the *Summary View* gave Jefferson "the reputation of a masterly pen" among Congress delegates in 1776 and won for the Virginian his assignment to draft the Declaration.

To the Williamsburg printer we owe a word of thanks for the important part that he has played in the affairs of this early Virginia capital—affairs that had notable influence on the course of American history. Since civilization began, the communication of ideas has largely depended upon the written word. The eighteenth-century printers of Williamsburg—and all America—served that need at a time of great moment, when the destiny of the emerging ideals of political democracy, free speech, a free press, and freedom of conscience was uncertain. They had the privilege of enlisting their craftsmanship in the service of freedom, peace, and plenty, goals that continue to beckon mankind.

To the printer's art, then, we wholeheartedly render the tribute which J. Markland pronounced in *Typographia*, in 1730, as he saluted Governor Gooch and Printer Parks for giving Virginia its first press:

> "*Happy the Art, by which we learn*
>
> *Gloss of Errors to detect,*
>
> *The Vice of Habits to correct,*
>
> *And sacred Truths, from Falsehood to discern!*
>
> *By which we take a far-stretch'd View,*
>
> *And learn our Fathers Vertues to pursue,*

Their Follies to eschew."

1730-1780

Milton Keynes UK
Ingram Content Group UK Ltd.
UKHW030720041024
449263UK00004B/340